CIVILIAN TO SOLDIER THROUGH COMBAT WWII
July 1943 – March 1946 AD

Carl R. Russell, Sr.

PublishAmerica
Baltimore

© 2010 by Carl R. Russell, Sr.
All rights reserved. No part of this book may be reproduced, stored in a retrieval system or transmitted in any form or by any means without the prior written permission of the publishers, except by a reviewer who may quote brief passages in a review to be printed in a newspaper, magazine or journal.

First printing

PublishAmerica has allowed this work to remain exactly as the author intended, verbatim, without editorial input.

Hardcover 978-1-4489-6491-8
Softcover 978-1-4489-7640-9
PAperback 978-1-4512-4579-0
PUBLISHED BY PUBLISHAMERICA, LLLP
www.publishamerica.com
Baltimore

Printed in the United States of America

DEDICATION

Dedicated to the memory of my mother who entered her bedroom closet regularly to pray for the safe return of her only child from battle.

ACKNOWLEDGMENT

To Daphne Marshall, Director of Resident services at Wesley Ridge Retirement Community in Reynoldsburg, Ohio, who encouraged me to share my writing with others.

TABLE OF CONTENTS

CHAPTER 1
CIVILIAN TO SOLDIER – WORLD WAR II..................................11

CHAPTER 2
BACK TO COLLEGE..15

CHAPTER 3
75TH INFANTRY DIVISION...17

CHAPTER 4
TRIP TO THE BATTLE FRONT...19

CHAPTER 5
GRANDMENIL...21

CHAPTER 6
ARDENNES FOREST..23

CHAPTER 7
LOST...31

CHAPTER 8
HOSPITAL...33

CHAPTER 9
VICTORY...35

CHAPTER 10
SCHEDULE FOR HOME...37

CHAPTER 11
BACK HOME...39

EPILOGUE...41

CIVILIAN TO SOLDIER THROUGH COMBAT WWII
July 1943 – March 1946 AD

Carl R. Russell, Sr.

CHAPTER 1
CIVILIAN TO SOLDIER – WORLD WAR II

In June 1943, I was 19 years old and had graduated from Tiffin Business College with a major in Business Administration. I returned to the family farm located near Findlay, Ohio. After receiving a welcome from Uncle Sam, I was sent to Camp Atterbury in Indiana for my initial indoctrination to Army life.

I was issued my uniform, had all the immunizations they could think of, and then assigned to a barracks. I knew nothing of the ways of the Army at this point. Every morning we would go into platoon formation and then were dismissed for breakfast. After breakfast, I would go to the Post Exchange (PX) or take a walk and then get ready for lunch, then to a movie or just lay down to rest and get ready for my evening meal. I began to think that Army life was not too bad. I asked one of the other recruits in the barracks: "Where do they get all the help for the extra jobs?" He said, "You'd better check the bulletin board…" My name had been listed for KP for a couple of days. They called the job Kitchen Police. That sounded rather important to me to be a policeman with only several days in the Army. I was to report to the kitchen at 5:00am. Upon my arrival, I was handed a big bucket of water and a mop and was told to start cleaning the area. At 8:00am, I was to report to the Company Commander. The Company Commander gave me a little explanation of Army rules and regulations. I was tempted to say that I wasn't deaf, but I held on. As a reward for failing to report the first days, I was assigned latrine duties for the rest of my time at this camp. I should have received a medal as the best toilet bowl cleaner in the whole Army!!

My next lesson in the Army was a call to guard duty. My first assignment was at night. We were supposed to follow a certain path and challenge anyone that crossed the path. Naturally, it was raining my first night on duty. Being my first introduction to Army discipline it seemed silly to me to walk around in the rain and get all wet! I found a good place to stay out of the rain and my intention was to get back to the starting point about the time I was supposed to be replaced by a new guard

I was relaxed in my cover until all of a sudden I heard someone shouting: "Sergeant of the Guard." My best laid plans of staying out of the rain were suddenly changed. I ran out to the route I was supposed to be on and immediately I had to challenge two people coming towards me. The first one was the Sergeant of the Guard and the second was a Colonel who happened to be the Camp Commander! The next few minutes were spent loudly talking about responsibility and discipline. I didn't contribute much to the conversation except, "Yes Sir" and "No Sir". The next item discussed was the length of jail sentence. Being already scheduled to be shipped out of Camp Atterbury to Camp Roberts, California, they agreed to let me continue what was quickly becoming a successful Army career.

It was a long trip by railroad from Camp Atterbury, Indiana to Camp Roberts, California. I had time to think about the War. Our country was fighting a war with Japan and with Germany. The need for trained men was enormous. Camp Roberts was an infantry replacement training center where the job was to get men ready for combat in a short period of time. My decision was to accept the fact that our country was at war and I had to do my part.

Upon my arrival at Camp Roberts, I was assigned to a Company and introduced to the Sergeant in charge. He promptly told us that we were the dumbest bunch of recruits that he ever tried to train. Some of the words he used would not be acceptable in church.

Our training started with long marches. Being in the infantry, we had to qualify in the use of M/1 rifles, light machine guns, 60 mm mortars, and the use of the bayonet. On the infiltration course, we had to move forward through mine fields and close overhead machine gun fire. This was to give us a preview of the sounds of combat. The last thing we did for graduation was a 20-mile march with full field packs. I had made the transition from a civilian to a soldier.

CHAPTER 2
BACK TO COLLEGE

My next adventure in the Army was a complete surprise! They told me I was going BACK TO COLLEGE. 'Get ready to leave'!!

Instead of going over to Europe or Japan as an infantry replacement, I was chosen to be in the Army Specialized Training Program. I can't think of any good reason for my appointment except perhaps the record I had in my previous Army experience. I was well on my way to earning a Good Conduct Medal!! Maybe they never looked at other records.

They sent me to Alfred University, New York, where I was enrolled in an engineering program. At the end of the quarter I was transferred to Manhattan College in New York. Without any warning, I was appointed temporary Captain and put in charge of all Army Units stationed at the school.

My weekends were spent on Broadway with all the shows and other activities. All soldiers were given special prices on all events. At the end of the quarter we were informed that the Army Specialized Training Program was terminated and we were to be transferred to the 75th Infantry Division now on maneuvers in Louisiana. My college vacation was over and I was back in the real Army!!

CHAPTER 3
75th INFANTRY DIVISION

The Army Specialized Training program was closed because of the need for men to replace wounded and those killed in action. Our country was fighting a war with Japan and in Europe. The need for trained men was enormous.

The 75th Infantry Division was formed to give help in defeating Germany. The division was nicknamed the "diaper division" because of the average age of the men.

My trip from New York to Louisiana was without problems. Upon our arrival, we were immediately told to get our field packs and get off the train. Naturally it was raining very hard so I was wanting to get to my shelter immediately. The sergeant just laughed at me and said, "Your tent is in the bag brought with you!"

I was trucked out to the location of my Company. I was assigned to the Weapon Platoon of Co. L: 3rd Battalion, 289th Regiment of the 75th Infantry Division.

It was still raining when I woke up the next morning but I had lots of company in my misery! It was time to get acquainted with the fellows in my platoon. These were people that I would be with for the balance of the war! I was designated to be in the mortar group of 60mm mortars – the weight was 40 lbs. each.

At the end of our training in Louisiana, the 75th was transferred to Camp Breckenridge, KY, where the final preparation was being made for overseas duty.

Camp Breckenridge was a good place for training officers and for keeping troops in good physical condition. One of the most frequent uses of time were long marches with full field packs. One of the first things they planned was to go on a ten mile march at night with all equipment. This did not appeal to me! When they started the march we had to answer to roll call. I answered "yes" when they called my name. I promptly went into the barracks to wait their return. Several hours later I heard them coming so I hurried out so I could answer roll call! All went as planned until I said "here" when they called my name. I heard a loud "Fall out!" from the First Sgt. With instructions to report to his office immediately. The First Sgt. had checked attendance at the end of five miles and, of course, I was in the barracks resting.

I spent the balance of my stay at the camp scrubbing floors on weekends and other free times. This was done until I was given one week furlough to visit home. They informed me that the Division was scheduled to ship out of the states to an unknown destination.

CHAPTER 4
TRIP TO THE BATTLE FRONT

On October 16, 1944 Company L left Camp Breckenridge by train and arrived at Camp Shanks, New York. We knew then that we were headed for Europe. On October 16th we boarded the HMT Franconia which was a freighter made over to carry troops. We were put in a convoy with ships like oil tankers so it was a slow journey. The Navy was responsible for guarding the convoy from submarines and mines. We were allowed two meals per day and were assigned to a table. After a couple of days at sea we had only five men that were able to eat because the rest were seasick. We still drew rations for twenty and the five of us were able to eat most of it. Being a British ship the menu included fish about ninety per cent of the time. We were all ways concerned about those who were on deck and unable to eat. We would take a slice of bread to the deck and they would head for the railing! We just wanted to be sure they were not hungry!

We arrived at Liverpool, England on November 14, 1944. We went by train to Camp Pretty, Penclawwd, Wales. On December 9, 1944 we left England on an LST and landed at LeHavre, France. The first thing I saw was a group of soldiers gathered around a fire to keep warm. They didn't know it, but the fire was built on an unexploded bomb. We saw our first casualties as we marched to our first camp in France.

On December 10, 1944 our Company moved to camp in Freeville, France. This is an area where I saw a cow in a field that needed to be milked. Since I was the only farm boy in our platoon I was elected to milk the cow. From that time on my name was Clem – the farmer. After a while I heard a shot and I figured out that the cow was to supply some meat. I had a hamburger and the officers had steak.

On December 16th, the German Army started what was to be known as the Battle of the Bulge. We had our last church service before leaving for the front. I promised my God to serve Him all my days if He spared my life and I have tried to fulfill that promise!

On December 17th our Division was immediately on the move toward the front. We were on an army truck moving at night. I went to sleep and my helmet fell off and left me no protection for my head! When I got off the truck, the driver, who was a black man, gave me his helmet! At this time we had no information about what was taking place in the battle. All we knew was that we were moved into the battle in a very short period of time. On December 23rd, we were moved to Briscol, Belgium. On December 24th we were on the road to Grandmenil. We noticed that the tanks and trucks were moving in the other direction. Late that day we made our first contact with the 2nd German Panzer Division.

CHAPTER 5
GRANDMENIL

This is a history of my own experiences in actual combat starting on December 24, 1944. Our Company L, along with K Company, was ordered to capture Grandmenil, Belgium because it was an important road junction and would stop the German push towards Leige, Belgium. Toward evening we were on the road approaching the town. What a way to spend the night before Christmas! We were marching along the road when I heard guns firing. I immediately went to the ditch along the side of the road. A Sherman tank plus eight Tiger tanks passed by my position without seeing me. I was about ready to move but somebody had called in fire from big guns so it was back to the ditch. As soon as that fire was lifted the tanks came back heading back to town. We lost our Company Commander and K Company lost quite a number of men. The tanks ran over our Jeep. We had to delay our push to Grandmenil.

On December 27th, our Company L was ordered to try again! I was assigned to go with the Third Platoon and to stay close to the Lieutenant. We were to cross a field toward the town. About half way across the field, enemy mortar shell lit beside the Lieutenant and blew his helmet off his head, but did not touch any other place! The helmet had a big gash cut in it. I was standing on the other side of the Lieutenant and had nothing hit me except the noise of the explosion. We ran into town! We were there, but so were the Germans! I was going up one of the streets and a German tank saw me from across the field. I knew I had about two or three seconds to react. I was next to a house and saw a door open so I dove into the kitchen and slid under the kitchen table as the wall fell and shrapnel scattered. I could hear other fellows screaming for a medic saying "They got Clem!" I came walking out of what was left of the house. It was beginning to get a little dark so I set my mortar to support the riflemen. I stood up to survey my surroundings and a sniper took a shot at my head and came so close to my ear that I could not hear right for several days. The rest of the night I threw up flares with the mortar to try to avoid a counter attack. Then the weather turned cold with temperatures of 0 to -20. The next day we went from house to house throwing hand grenades to clean up the town. The cold weather continued at 0 to -20 and snow started to fall – turning into blizzard conditions as we left Grandmenil.

CHAPTER 6
ARDENNES FOREST

The next battle I remember was a forced march through days of snow. The Germans were starting to retreat and some General thought it would be good strategy to surround the next town and trap one of their divisions. We had no preparation time but started immediately. We had no food with us and snow had to be our water supply. We marched night and day without rest. By the second night going through the Ardennes Forest, we started to run into booby traps and land mines. The person ahead would point out trip wires as we moved ahead. It was difficult to see them because of the snow and it was night. The Corporal just ahead of me caught his foot on a trip wire to set off what they call a Bouncing Betty. It goes about five feet in the air and a load of dynamite explodes. I was at right angle and it did not affect anything but my hearing. The medics came up and carried off the Corporal. We started on through the woods and by the third night, we were wading snow hip deep and still without food. Men started to fall down from exhaustion. We had to take turns beating them to keep circulation going and get them on their feet. We finally arrived at our destination after three days and nights of marching. The Germans had gone! They pulled us off the line and brought up our kitchens to feed us and to get cleaned up. The food did very little good because the stomach had shrunk and could hold no food. It took several days to recover. At the end of the week, we were on the move ready to chase the Germans!

Taken July 21, 1943, the day before leaving for the Army.

Camp Breckinridge, KY in training, 1944

CAMP BRECKINRIDGE, KY. IN TRAINING 1944

Honeymoon – June 1948

Church building in Granmenil where sniper had fired at me

My hand on a German tank in Granmenil, Belgium, 1988

CHAPTER 7
LOST

After a couple of days to recuperate, we were ordered back to the front. The movement of troops was generally at night. Our Squad got lost and we ended up on the German side. We were in a town and were not sure which way to go. I was standing with one foot upon the curb of the street. I heard a strange click and then a 37mm shell from an anti-tank gun came at me. It had a red glow which meant it was an armor piercing shell. It went between my legs hitting the curb where my foot was and went on through the air making a lot of noise. We immediately broke a door down in the nearest house and held hostage an older man, his wife, and a daughter. We searched the house for German soldiers and then agreed to stay there until morning so we could see who had control of that part of the town. At about ten in the morning we saw American soldiers coming down the street. We went out to meet them and to ask if they knew where

Company L of the 289th Regiment might be located. They pointed to another part of the area surrounding the town. We located 3rd Battalion headquarters and they told us that Company L was on the other side of Suicide Hill and it was best to wait until dark to get their location. I did not want to wait until dark to get to Company L so I asked them to point out the direction. Suicide Hill was land free of trees and on the top of the hill was a path leading to the other side. The Germans had mortars and 88's zeroed in on the path. The path was about as long as a football field is wide – about 50 feet. I took off at full speed. I probably would have broken the record for the mile run if we had just had an official record keeper on duty! The Germans were so surprised that they did not fire a single shot. The rest of my group followed. I headed for the Company L headquarters, which was in a house. On the way, I passed Lieutenant Usher who was responsible for placement of mortars and machine guns talking with a Sergeant from another platoon. Even though Lieutenant Usher was in charge of our group, I did not stop to talk with him but went straight to the house to rest and pick up supplies. I heard a large blast from outside the house. The report came to us that Lieutenant Usher and the Sergeant had been killed by a mortar shell. We were ordered to take the town and were successful but it cost us the largest number of killed in action and wounded of any battle we had fought.

CHAPTER 8
HOSPITAL

The fight to restore original battle lines before the Bulge was ended in success for the 75th Division. The Division was called to southern France to help for what was to be called the Colmar Pocket battle. The winter weather experienced in the Battle of the Bulge was the most severe winter that Europe had in many years. In addition to deep snow, the temperature would be 0 degrees to -20. On January 27th, just before we were to ship out to southern France, I came down with a high temperature and a medic sent me directly to the hospital near Leige, Belgium. As I remember, the hospital was in a regular building and not a tent. There were plenty of nurses and doctors available. The place seemed to be very busy and every room was filled with wounded soldiers. I was placed in the overflow – which meant a hallway. It was also crowded with just enough space for doctors and nurses to go from one patient to another. I was diagnosed with pneumonia and poor circulation in my feet. The foot problem was due to my inability to remove my combat boots while in battle combined with the extreme cold weather. Now, an interesting cure was developed concerning the pneumonia. A scientist in England had just developed a drug called penicillin. It was used in my case, and worked for a very quick and complete cure of the pneumonia. It took extra weeks to regain my full strength because of the kind and lack of food while in combat. By the last of February I rejoined my Company on the bank of the Rhine River.

CHAPTER 9
VICTORY

The assignment that was given to our mortar group early in the month of March was to dig a huge foxhole on the bank of the Rhine River. We were given 50 mm machine guns in addition to our 60 mm mortars. They gave us steel plates to cover the hole that we had made. We were to observe activity on the other side of the river and give them reason to be careful! One thing that happened during one of my night watches was a noise that sounded like rain on the river, yet it was not raining. I thought the Germans must be coming. All of a sudden, it dawned on me that U.S. bombers overhead were dropping small pieces of aluminum to confuse radars. Soon we found out why our preparations had been so elaborate. On the 26th of March at 1:00pm, the 9th Army Commander scheduled a 1600 gun barrage in preparation for the 9th Army to cross the Rhine. There was always danger of short rounds in a concentrated use of artillery.

On the 29th of the month, our Division crossed over the river on a pontoon bridge near Lohrhor and the battle of the Ruhr had started for our Division. We went from town to town picking up prisoners and getting local government back working. Our part of the battle ended on the 18th of April. VE day came on the 8th day of May. The 75th Division was moved back to Leon, France!

CHAPTER 10
SCHEDULE FOR HOME

After the defeat of Germany and Japan, every soldier was anxious to go home. They assigned part of our Division to help in scheduling departures from Europe to the United States. Our unit was moved to a camp near Rheims, France soon after the war ended. They discovered that I knew how to type so I was not listed on the "Home Soon" list. About July of that year (1945), my cousin, who had fought in Italy and southern France, visited our Camp on a four day leave. We had not seen each other since March 1943.

Our unit continued to process soldiers to go home until about October 1945 and we were told our part of the work was finished and ordered to close the Camp. All were transferred except a Lieutenant, a Sergeant, and myself. The Lieutenant signed a blank form because he was in a hurry to go home. The

Sergeant and I filled the blank paper authorizing us to have a jeep and we made our travel itinerary so we would end up in Paris, which had to be our final destination. Our first stop was the U.S.O. in Brussels, Belgium. We were at a dance that night, and I suppose the girl I danced with still has foot trouble! I don't remember any other part of the trip, but we ended at Eisenhower's headquarters in Paris. I finally had my orders to go home in March 1946!

CHAPTER 11
BACK HOME

I was transferred to a port in LeHavre, France and boarded a Navy vessel for the trip home. We had a smooth start and I was enjoying the trip until someone told me I had to do KP duty for the navy. We got about half way to New York and ran into a hurricane! The ship was small and we were tossed around like a cork. Some mechanical difficulty occurred because of the storm. The ship would roll from side to side and it was almost impossible to stand at a table and eat. It was one of those days I was on KP. I saw the Navy Captain coming through the kitchen and I happened to have a pail of garbage in my possession. On a hard roll of the ship, I lost control of the garbage to accidentally soak the Captain. I felt better about KP.

The movie star, Mickey Rooney, was with us on the trip home. I had him put his name on a dollar bill as a souvenir. I lost it before I reached home. We landed in New York and was greeted by a U.S.O. worker who asked me if I wanted a drink of milk. I had not had good milk since leaving the U.S.A. I promptly consumed two quarts!

I was discharged from the Army on March 6, 1946. One of my first visits after coming home was to visit the most beautiful girl in the world – whose picture I had carried with me all during the war – Mary. By June of 1948, I had convinced her to be my wife. That life together would make another book about being happy! If you remember, I asked the Lord to save my life in combat and I would serve Him all my days. Together Mary and I have endeavored to put the Lord first in everything we have done in this life!

EPILOGUE

In 1988, forty-two years after returning from Europe, Mary and I traveled to Germany. One of our daughters was living near Frankfurt where her husband was stationed at the U.S. Air Force base. They were expecting their first child who arrived the day after we did!

Two weeks later our youngest daughter, who had been with her sister, joined us and our son-in-law on a drive to Belgium. We headed toward Granmenil where I first went into battle on December 24, 1944. The town was renamed on the map but when we finally stopped to ask directions from a roadside food vendor our daughter, speaking French, could converse with him and found we were only 50-75 feet from the road leading into the town. When we turned up that road and I looked to my right, I saw the field where we advanced into town and the road where the eight German tanks had plowed thru our Company

L. My wife told me later she had never seen her husband as I became in that moment exclaiming over and over – "That's the field! That's the field!"

As we went into the village, one of the first sights we saw was a German tank left by the town as a reminder of the war. We walked down the street to the church building where from the belfry the sniper had shot so closer to my ear. Walking farther down the street I was reminded of the German tank fire that caused me to dive into the house before the shell exploded and the house collapsed on top of the table where I took refuge. We knocked on a door and a young man, wearing a miller's apron, answered. He could not understand English or French but when I said "American Soldat – German Soldat!" the light came on in his eyes and he grabbed my hand in a hearty shake!

Later at the Bastogne Memorial, a middle aged man approached and asked if I had been in the war. When I said I had he grabbed my hand and with tears in his eyes said, "We love you Americans for what you did for us!" Later, as we walked the grounds and we saw one another, he saluted me.

Ten years later thru the 75th Infantry organization, I was able to contact and visit with two of the men who had been buddies throughout the war experiences. We had not seen each other in over fifty years and it was a joyous reunion!

Carl R. Russell, Sr.
Age 85
September 2009 AD

CPSIA information can be obtained at www.ICGtesting.com
Printed in the USA
LVOW08s2139301213

367523LV00001B/77/P